ENDINGS: POETRY AND PROSE

ENDINGS: POETRY AND PROSE

WILLIAM POE

Copyright © 2015 William Poe

ISBN-13: 9781516836932
ISBN-10: 1516836936
Library of Congress Control Number: 2015915662

Independently Published: Kindle Direct Publishing

ART

JASPER'S FINE ART

Jasper's thesis advisor had rejected all his ideas, and so he was desperate to think up another. His acquisition of a master's degree in fine arts depended on it. Jasper's plan had been to stage a traditional show and display his abstract paintings in a local gallery. But the thesis advisor held that painting was dead and further that Jasper's abstract style was an exhausted visual language. Jasper had lost the argument that if that were true, then no one would need bother to write a play, since Shakespeare had explored all the possibilities of English drama.

While sitting in a lecture about writing science proposals, an idea came to Jasper. It occurred to him that a hypothesis could become the basis of a conceptual art piece. Conducting an experiment under the guise of art might be just the thing to impress his advisor. Jasper presented the idea, and the advisor approved.

After getting a special permit from the city, Jasper arranged for a notice to be published in the local newspaper announcing the intention of Jasper Jones, a local art student, to organize an art happening along two blocks of Main Street. When the day arrived, a crowd of several dozen people, mostly students from the art department, gathered along the sidewalks. Jasper selected volunteers and told them not what would be required, only that they would be fitted with cardboard helmets that limited their line of sight. Jasper painted colorful abstract designs on the helmets.

Before he started the performance, Jasper distributed flyers explaining the concept and the expected outcome. The three volunteers would walk side by side, unable to see the hands of the others. In addition, they would be listening to music through headphones in order to eliminate aural cues.

The experiment was designed to test what Carl Jung called "supraconsciousness," an awareness that brings people into harmony despite the laws of probability, which would predict randomness. In the handout, Jasper cited various philosophers whose ideas could be used to support the argument that humans are more than automatons in a senseless universe.

"The performance you are about to witness will demonstrate that we are one in the game of Art-and-Life," stated the flyer, whose banner read, "The P-S-R Phenomenon As It Applies to Supraconscious Reality."

As the volunteers got ready, Jasper gave each a slip of paper with instructions on how to begin.

"Start with paper," the first volunteer was told. "Start with scissors," the second was instructed. The final volunteer was told, "Begin with rock."

"One, two, three, go!" Jasper announced loudly so the audience would hear. He alerted the participants with hand signals. Jasper walked beside the trio, recording the event on video. When they reached the goal, a white chalk line that Jasper had drawn from curb to curb, the volunteers stopped and held out their hands.

As predicted, each one displayed the hand signal for paper.

The witnesses gathered around to see the result. Some were amazed; others were incredulous. Jasper ran the experiment twice more. The second time he started with scissors—which were displayed by each volunteer at the completion the walk. The third, predictably, started and ended with rock.

All the bystanders gasped at the third outcome. In the final cut of his video, Jasper spliced together their many astonished expressions. He presented the work to the thesis advisor, who brought it before a panel that would decide Jasper's future as an artist. The panel granted Jasper his MFA.

After receiving his degree, Jasper returned to abstract painting. Without exception, gallery owners rejected his works. They all knew of the "Paper-Scissors-Rock Phenomenon"—it had been posted on YouTube—and asked why he was not pursuing what they thought would be a promising career as a conceptual artist. Several gallery owners offered to sponsor a new happening.

After a few years surviving as a clerk at Walmart during the day and painting late into the night, Jasper moved to Washington, DC, to live with a cousin. His MFA degree and experience as a clerk helped him land a job in the registrar's office of the Smithsonian's National Air and Space Museum. He hoped that in such a sophisticated city where so many people worked for museums he might finally get a one-person show. Jasper had amassed a large collection of works by that time. Many hung on the walls of a studio he rented in Washington's Takoma neighborhood.

Jasper joined art groups and went to openings, where he handed out business cards to anyone who would accept them. When no one called, he decided to participate in the unjuried Artomatic exhibition, which accepted entries on a first-come, first-served basis. He decided to hang a wall-sized work he recently completed, a painting full of resplendent colors splashed on the canvas with bold sweeps of the arm. Jasper was sure that the work would draw attention. Gallery owners ridiculed Artomatic; nevertheless, they toured the show.

Near Jasper's monumental painting, another entrant had installed the very type of "art" that Jasper abhorred. Jasper had, in fact, chosen his spot because he could not imagine anyone being interested in the installation. It featured a couch with a bicycle contraption placed in front where one could position his or her feet and work the pedals. That "manual labor" drove a fan placed in a hollowed-out air conditioner about ten feet away. Air blew toward the person while a mock tornado siren blared. A sign on the wall explained that the energy used to cool our houses hurt the earth, just as pedaling the bicycle from such an awkward position caused leg pain. The work was hailed by a critic from the *Washington Post* as an "evocative, sensory experience that brought art into the realm of ecological consciousness."

No one commented on Jasper's work, *A Passage to Oblivion*.

The experience at Artomatic made Jasper more determined than ever. He took stock of his work and found that he had nearly two hundred paintings. The smallest of them measured three by four feet. He hired a competent photographer and made a website for his art. He spent several thousand dollars to have a high-gloss brochure designed and printed. He took the brochure, along with a dozen color prints, to every gallery in Washington, convinced that the problem had been his lack of initiative and not the quality of his art.

One gallery seemed an especially good prospect because many of the works hanging on the walls resembled his own. The owner asked Jasper about previous exhibitions he had entered. She told him to return after he had been awarded one or two first-place prizes. That was her minimum criterion for accepting new artists.

At another gallery, Jasper was told that he could not be considered a professional artist since he was not at his craft on a full-time basis. The owner told Jasper that he was the type of amateur that collectors avoided.

And so it went with every gallery. After three weeks of rejection, Jasper was about to give up, but he decided to try one last gallery that was open by appointment only. When he spoke to the owner, he vaguely suggested that he was a collector and needed a work appraised. Jasper dressed in his finest suit and bought a black leather portfolio to display prints of his paintings. He was sure the owner would forgive the ruse.

The gallery was on the ground floor of a townhouse in DuPont Circle. When Jasper opened the portfolio for the woman and began turning the pages, she made several positive comments, which gave Jasper hope.

"This one is very nice," the woman said of the painting that so many had overlooked at the Artomatic show. "It's a strong piece. The rhythms remind me of the late Jackson Pollock."

Jasper smiled as he turned to the last page and said, "If you like Pollock, you will see how his early work influenced me. It isn't the same, of course, but doesn't this one, *Guardians of the Little Window*, remind you of *She-Wolf*?

"Oh dear," the woman said, "Didn't anyone tell you?"

"No," Jasper said, "tell me what?"

"I only sell works by dead artists."

Jasper closed his portfolio, slipped on his overcoat, and marched to the exit. The woman opened the door for him. As Jasper crossed the threshold, she started to say something but held back. Jasper left the gallery feeling like an impostor.

So many of the artists that Jasper admired had brief but intense careers and left behind great works of art as evidence of their passions. It had always haunted Jasper that Vincent van Gogh painted his best works during the last two years of his life. Like that famous artist, Jasper had only one brother, who, though they rarely saw each other, had always encouraged him in his endeavors.

For the next few weeks, Jasper inventoried his paintings, drawings, and the few sculptures he had constructed. He chronicled each according to the date of completion as best as he could recall and made sure each piece was signed. He composed a note that explained who he was and why his output should matter to the history of art. Then he placed all the works in a storage unit that he pre-paid for a month, which was all he could afford after preparing the expensive portfolio.

Though he never doubted the quality of his work, Jasper had started to doubt his role in society. He would make one last overture to the art world in hopes of saving what truly mattered—his paintings. Though he would be compromising his principles, as he had in order to achieve his MFA, he anticipated no condemnation for enacting the ultimate performance.

In his efforts to find a gallery, Jasper had amassed a sizeable mailing list; it included the names and addresses of everyone in the Washington metropolitan area who supported the arts. Jasper sent letters to everyone in his file. Nothing remained but the method of execution. Jasper abhorred guns, and he was sure that his physician would refuse to prescribe a medication strong enough to stop his heart. The answer came to him after reading a newspaper article about a man suspected by the FBI of being responsible for the 2001 anthrax attacks. After being accused, the man killed himself by taking an overdose of Tylenol.

It can never be known whether Jasper's art could have revived the style he loved so much. His art remained unseen. The letter he sent to his brother asking that he take responsibility for Jasper's many works of art left in storage was lost in the mail. Months passed before the authorities could locate the brother to bring the news that Jasper had committed suicide. The storage unit had been auctioned, and the disappointed buyer hauled Jasper's art to the dump. The gallery owners, critics, and newspaper editors who received his mailing thought it was a prank. Only a few, after they read about Jasper in the obituaries, remembered the last line of the letter they had received:

"My final performance demonstrates that we are one in the game of art— and death."

CANVAS IS A PLACE

Canvas is a place,
somewhere I go alone.
There I meet the unknown
the faraway
the deep within.

Sometimes, I meet a person there.
At times I am consumed
and confusion addresses me.
Then I must struggle
to the surface.

I always go again,
compelled by what I don't know
and can't understand.
Expelled from this place,
I am always welcome there—
even to stay and never return.

Paint is a medium
who speaks in trance
and obscures the real.
Her voice eats my eyes
and burns my brain.
The medium holds me
in her stare.
I resist, only to make
love to her once again.

One day I will
be the canvas and paint
and stay
where I will go alone.

THE CULT OF PAINTING

I belong to the cult of painting
and worship the gods of color;
they manufacture the world
and provide a pulse for life.

I have accepted Creative Power
and give life by what I do.
The easel is my altar
and the canvas a holy shroud.

I have learned the theology of brushes
and know the discipline of the knife;
I am the leader and the follower,
and together we rule the world.

THE STOIC

Hey, Stoic,
Once upon a time a few months ago,
we were in bed messing around.
Then one day you didn't know me;
to my perception you had bottled
yourself up again,
the way you were when I met you.
Then it was the drugs;
now it's the pseudoreligion
you chose to take its place.
Today you broke down a tiny bit
and agreed to look at my new paintings.
They are pure emotion—
raw, unbridled, overwhelming—
you couldn't look at them.
You actually could not look at them.
Then I showed you one painting a little
less emotional, and you made some insignificant
comment.
Can't you look inside anymore.

What you hide within will eat its way out;
what I held at bay is coming out as passion
in my paintings.
You, Mister Stoic, don't let yours come out in death.

NOT SYLVIA PLATH

I am not Sylvia Plath,
and not Edgar Allan Poe;
but what I am, I fought for to the death.
Today, listening to a story about Plath, I kept
thinking of Anne Sexton, and about the fifties,
and Modernism and mentorship, about fame and
Smith College. Then I looked in the mirror
and saw only me.

No one taught me to write or read or holler
out from the depths of my despair.
One day I awoke, and the screams were there,
adolescent, perhaps, but just as painful as
a pampered poem.

THERE WAS A MAN

There was a man who worked
and ran
when he stopped he started up again
running in circles
running with purpose
determined sleepwalk running
he worked with colleagues
impressed for all their specialization
he could whirl their thoughts
and words into processed forms
full of fonts and attributes
the man worked hard
specialization bored him
he ran then worked for specialists
because he has to do something
when he can't sleep and can't run

one day the man painted

now the paintings run for him
as he sleeps

ACTS OF BEAUTY

The little boy sought to please
producing acts of beauty
with ease,
his heart filled with simple joy
delighting in creation like a toy,
the wonderment and mystery of a line
of a poem,
the brilliance and thrill of color
in a painting's shimmering hue or shade
bursting with pride
at what he had made.

"Mother, mother, look what I've done,
look what has come through my hands."

A child's offering
presented
to a god.
Thundering deep within his soul
her response,
"It's stupid, it's odd."

DEATH

THE TIGER BOY

People often said that Timon was a smart boy. Even so, he was told that he would have to repeat the second grade. Timon walked with his dog around the backyard of his rural home and wondered what he'd done wrong. He believed what people said about his being smart. He had proven it.

When Timon was just three and a half years old, his grandmother, who lived with his family, took Timon on a shopping trip to downtown Little Rock. Timon used Crayons to fill in a coloring book during the ride on the county bus. After Timon's grandmother bought a new dress at Blass's Department Store on Main Street, they began walking to Pfeifer's Department Store, three blocks away. His grandmother suddenly collapsed on the sidewalk. Timon didn't witness the fall directly; he caught a reflection of the event in the window of the drugstore where they were planning to stop for a soda. People gathered quickly; there were men in black coats with narrow ties and women wearing small velvet hats adorned with colored feathers, some with gaudy flowers and hatpins—hatpins were common.

"What's your name, little boy?" someone asked.

Another questioned, "Do you know your name?"

Timon was smart; how could he not know his name?

"I'm Timon," he said forthrightly, "*Ti-mun*, and that's my grandma."

Someone telephoned for help. Distant sirens pierced the noise of cars and buses passing on the street. Most of the onlookers went about their business. A few remained to wait with him. Timon wondered why no one asked him how to reach his mother. Her number was firmly lodged in his memory.

Timon had watched his mother pick up their home phone's heavy receiver, twirl her index finger in the circles, and magically reach another person. His mother often held the receiver to his ear so he could talk to aunts and uncles.

Then she said, "Remember this number, Timon: four-five-four-oh-six. Someone where I work will answer on the other end."

Timon looked at the crowd surrounding him and said loudly, "Does anyone want the number?"

A kindly old woman who had decided to remain with him until the ambulance arrived said, "What is it, little boy? What are you trying to say?"

"It's four-five-four-oh-six."

"Land sakes alive!" the woman exclaimed. "This little boy knows his phone number."

"Someone will answer where my momma works," Timon said proudly. "That's the number."

"Let me go dial it," a businessman offered. He repeated the number back to Timon. When the little boy nodded, the man went into the drugstore. He remained visible through the window as he approached the soda jerk at the counter. The two then disappeared into a back room. By the time the man returned, Timon's grandmother was beginning to stir. The moment she opened her eyes, she protested about the fuss people were making.

"The boy's mother is on the way," the man told those still gathered as he came from the store. It was lunchtime, and no one wanted to dawdle if they weren't needed.

Timon's grandmother was a proud woman who refused to accept that she was in her eighties. In her mind, she was no older than fifty-five. Asked about her age, she had given the same answer for decades.

Just as the ambulance arrived, Timon's grandmother managed to get to her feet with the assistance of the businessman and the woman. The paramedics waited for Timon's mother, who pulled up behind the ambulance and raced from the car.

"Timy," she called, using Timon's nickname.

Timon felt proud of the fact that he had remembered the number she gave him. He shot his mother a toothy grin as she approached.

The woman and the businessman patted Timon on the head. "You're a smart little boy," the woman said.

Timon shrugged. He was straining to listen as his mother scolded his grandmother for bringing him into town.

The shopping incident seemed like the distant past by the time Timon finally started third grade. He retained a vague sense of the pride he had felt. The shopping trip was the last one for his grandmother after Timon's father moved the family from a small house in Little Rock to a much larger one in an unincorporated area of the county. Timon was three at the time of the move. His mother commuted to Little Rock. She worked as a bookkeeper at Wright's Auto Service Company on Broadway. His father was a carpenter who travelled the county as opportunities arose. In the years since he learned his first phone number, the numbers had grown longer. Now they included words. In the city, they began with FRanklin or MOhawk or CApital. People living in the rural community had LOcust as a prefix. Timon remembered every number he heard.

Having lived all her life in the city and now unable to go shopping, Timon's grandmother withdrew into a state of perpetual melancholy. Her fainting spells began occurring with such regularity that Timon's mother confined her to the house. On one occasion, she ventured into the backyard. Timon found his grandmother sprawled on the ground. He let her lie there until his mother came home. He was afraid his grandmother had died, and he didn't want to touch a dead body.

When Timon started school, instead of the word *smart*, Timon heard other words being used to describe him. His teacher told Timon's father (within earshot of Timon) that he could read well enough, but that he didn't comprehend the meaning of the words. Timon was slow to realize the connection between the printed word and those spoken aloud.

A few weeks prior to summer vacation, the principal summoned Timon to his office. His father was there.

"Your son needs to repeat the third grade, just as he did the second," the principal said, glancing at Timon.

Timon's father thought he had left the building site where he was working to hear that his son had improved. He had been telling people how good his boy was with numbers.

"Are you saying there's something wrong with my boy?" Timon's father protested.

The principal defended his position, pointing to comments on lessons he had taken from Timon's file. They said that Timon had "comprehension problems." He also needed to improve his social skills. Timon's father grew angry, and he told the principal to hire better teachers.

As the argument grew more heated, Timon took a ballpoint pen from his Mickey Mouse lunch pail and began to draw flying saucers and bug-eyed monsters on the palm of his hand, and rolling up his sleeve, he extended the scene up his inner arm until he ran out of skin. The two men didn't notice. Timon had gotten clever about concealing his drawing habit. He'd gotten in trouble at home for scribbling on the front door. Then he found that he could safely draw on the baseboard behind the curtains or on the wooden panels near the floor behind the furniture. Whole scenes, rendered in crayon, could be seen on the baseboard behind the bureau in the dining room. When his mother scolded him for covering his forehead with spirals, Timon started to draw on hidden areas of his body. That time in the principal's office was the first example of using his forearm as a canvas.

Timon's father couldn't convince the principal to advance his son to fourth grade. Timon spent a worried summer, not knowing what to expect as the neighborhood boys started to talk about the team sports they would be playing in the fourth grade. He understood that the principal was refusing to let him follow the other boys into the next grade, but he didn't understand why.

People began to treat Timon as though he didn't understand anything. They forgot about his ability to recall numbers. That particular talent didn't seem to matter anymore. In Timon's own mind, however, he continued to be smart.

When the neighborhood children taunted him that summer, circling him in a field and shouting, "Timon, Timon, broke a hymen, made the girls all cry," he knew what it meant. His older sister had used the word *hymen*, telling him that on a couple's honeymoon, the husband broke it and made his wife bleed by pushing himself between her legs. The idea scared Timon.

Timon stayed indoors the rest of the summer. His grandmother read to him, mostly nursery rhymes and limericks. One night, when he saw a comedian throw a plate of meringue at the host of a television show, he wondered about the line from one of the poems his grandmother read to him: "Simple Simon met a pieman." Timon especially remembered the last verse of the poem. It ended with Simple Simon bidding the world adieu. His grandmother had explained that "adieu" was "good-bye" in another language. As young as he was, Timon sometimes thought it might not be so bad to say good-bye and just disappear like Simple Simon.

With only two weeks remaining before school started, Timon's father explained that he would be going to fourth grade at a *parochial* school in the city. The Lutheran Church that ran the institution had accepted twice the annual fee to advance Timon. Timon didn't understand the word *parochial*, but he realized the school was far away and that he wouldn't know anyone there.

The school was in a building adjacent to a stone church. The room for fourth graders smelled old and musty. The lift-top desks had already survived many generations of students. The desks had inkwells, which now served as pencil holders. Within the first week, Timon thought he had made a friend, but the boy had only been acting friendly to collect information. When, in confidence, Timon told the boy about the chant, "Timon, Timon, broke a hymen," the supposed friend burst out laughing.

"You really are a simpleton, aren't you?" he said. He then bent toward Timon and jeered, "'Timon, Timon, broke a hymen.' Do you even know what that means?"

Timon shrugged. "I guess so."

The jeering boy took Timon's hand firmly and led him to the boys' restroom. He pushed Timon into a stall.

"This is what breaks it," the boy said, exposing himself and pressing against Timon like a nail going into his flesh.

Timon didn't understand. He began to cry, pulling up his pants and pushing past the boy to make it into the hallway.

During recess, the students teased Timon relentlessly. After two unendurable days, Timon told the teacher he had a stomachache. He was allowed to remain inside during recess. After that, Timon came down with an increasing variety of ailments. The only time Timon willingly joined his classmates was when the teacher led them on field trips to the library, two blocks away. Timon had begun to comprehend that books told stories, even better ones than his grandmother read to him.

Because he read so much, Timon started to understand more words than most fourth graders. He no longer received comments on his lesson sheets about reading problems. The new word that described his problems was *deportment*. Timon's hypochondria and unwillingness to play with the other children led to his teacher giving him poor marks for social skills.

His parents told Timon that he had to start getting along better with his classmates. Timon didn't know what to do. The other boys tried to hurt him when he joined their games. He had been cornered in the bathroom several times, sometimes by older, sixth-grade boys. He didn't like to think about what they did to him, and he never told anyone. Timon's parents frowned when they saw the unsatisfactory grade in deportment. Timon believed that was the reason his parents ignored him after they returned home from work.

The only way Timon could get their attention was to do something bad. And yet it was in Timon's nature to be a good boy. Timon often sat at his mother's feet as he read his books. She didn't acknowledge him. When he read out loud, she shushed him. One day, Timon accidentally knocked a potted plant off the end table. His mother scolded him, but at least that was attention. He sometimes took the family parakeet out of its cage. When his mother opened the front door, Timon threw the bird into the air. It made its way to freedom. Timon's mother had cooed at the bird every morning before going to work, speaking in a tone of voice that Timon envied. When she now awoke to the empty cage, she pursed her lips at Timon and frowned.

Nothing got the attention of Timon's father. Timon thought he was like the God who was mentioned in church, always there but never taking an active role in daily life. Clever Timon nonetheless managed to find ways to get close to his father. In the mornings, his father used a half bath adjacent to the kitchen. Pretending to get a glass of milk, Timon would open and then close the refrigerator door. He then had an excuse to be close to the bathroom without it seeming strange, and he could listen to the clinking of his father's razor hitting against the edge of the sink. Timon breathed in hard to get a whiff of the Old Spice aftershave that his father slapped on his face. The morning routine became so familiar that Timon knew exactly how long he could stand outside the bathroom before his father flushed the toilet, signaling the end of his morning preparations. Timon would then rush into the dining room where his bowl of cereal awaited him.

Timon would sneak back to the half bath one last time before his mother drove him to the parochial school. He had begun to collect his father's spent razor blades, retrieving them from the trash. Timon had long been drawn to sharp objects. When he couldn't sleep, he sometimes took a kitchen knife to bed. He associated the knife with preparations for the evening meal, and so he felt closer to his mother. Sometimes it made him remember the feeling of the nail piercing into his flesh and he used the knife in a similar way.

Timon stored dozens of his father's used razor blades in a special box hidden beneath a wooden panel in his closet. He had once cut his finger before learning how to handle the razor blades. He'd been fascinated by the clean gash, studying scientifically the way blood poured out when he pulled it open, and how it stopped when he applied pressure.

Timon's older sister had long since consigned her doll collection to the basement. Timon found the dolls one day and got an idea. He took each doll and looked it over as a surgeon might examine a patient on an operating table. One doll had an especially prominent nose. With a laugh, Timon sliced it off. He laughed even harder when he saw that the head was hollow. Remembering the older boys who cornered him in the school lavatory, Timon pulled down his pants and stuck his penis in the doll's head. He lay on the basement floor and laughed until he couldn't stop. When he gained composure, he tried to cut open the area between the doll's legs, but the plastic was too hard for the razor blade. He made a small cut on the tip of his index finger and smeared blood on the doll, wondering if that was what it looked like when "Timon broke a hymen."

He maimed all the dolls. Soon, his razor blades became dull. He became frustrated when he wasn't able to cut through a chubby arm, so he went upstairs and retrieved the kitchen knife. Now the arm came off as easily as slicing a carrot. Dolls' heads began to fall to the floor like French royalty sent to the guillotine. Legs required more hacking, but the effort gave Timon a thrill. Baby-doll drumsticks littered the floor around him. He grew sad when there were no more dolls.

During the summer following fourth grade, while his father and mother were at work and his grandmother was napping, Timon took that morning's razor blade and sliced into a pair of old shoes his mother had discarded, which he had rescued from the garbage. The act gave him a sense of closeness—almost a bodily connection—to his mother and father.

The day before the start of fifth grade, Timon took a razor blade outside and ran it along the siding above the brick foundation. The line was shallow, and no one noticed it. But Timon knew it was there, and it gave him a sense of ownership.

Timon began to need his razor blades to be with him at all times. He wrapped several in a paper towel and kept them in his pocket. Knowing he had the blades made him feel secure. Once, his teacher came up from behind and found Timon examining the blades at his desk. Realizing what Timon had in his hands, she backed away. Timon imagined himself turning into a tiger and growing razor-blade claws. He thought about it but didn't try to lunge at the teacher. After her initial hesitation, the teacher boldly took the blades from Timon and marched him to the principal's office. The man took a paddle out of a desk drawer, bent Timon over his knee, and smacked him hard on the thighs.

The teacher never imagined that Timon would bring more razor blades to school. But possessing them gave Timon the strength to endure. He wrapped individual blades in toilet paper and hid them in his socks. He stopped talking to everyone, even when the teacher asked him questions. His grades in deportment remained unsatisfactory.

Timon didn't pay attention when classmates taunted him. He could no longer remember what had happened when the older boys cornered him in the restroom. At home, Timon sat in front of the television and disappeared into whatever show caught his attention. He especially liked *Dobie Gillis* and was fond of the beatnik character, Maynard G. Krebs. In one episode, Maynard wore a tiger stripe vest. Timon wanted one just like it.

During class, when the teacher gave reading assignments, Timon instead drew pictures in the margins. The teacher demanded that Timon write a thousand times, "I will not draw pictures during class," but Timon ignored the punishment and got into more trouble as a result. The principal sent him home with a note saying that Timon was suspended for a day. When his mother asked what he had done to deserve the suspension, Timon didn't answer. He stood frozen, fingering a bare razor blade he had in his pocket.

Following the suspension, Timon was required to stay inside during recess for a few days so that he could make up his reading assignments. He began exploring the room, lifting the wooden top of the desk used by a girl he particularly disliked. He examined every item and then decided to steal her Pink Pet eraser. She had written her name on it. That night, alone in his room, Timon sliced into the eraser. The material was easier to cut than the dolls he had maimed. It was more like the way it felt when he cut his finger. The Pink Pet eraser became a pile of skin-like membranes. Timon wasn't satisfied. He needed to cut into something else. He pulled open one of his dresser drawers and sliced off splinters from the wood at the back. When bedtime came, he stuffed the slivers of wood into his pillowcase and went to sleep.

After he caught up with his assignments, Timon intentionally got into trouble so he would be made to stay inside. Over the course of a week, Timon had taken all the erasers from the other students' desks. At night, Timon locked himself in his room and cut them into slices.

It was a relief when the weekend arrived. Timon had taken so many erasers that he was certain to be found out. He needed a miracle. And for once, one arrived—at least it seemed that way to Timon. Timon's mother got a salary bonus, cash given to workers with young children. She took Timon to shop for clothes. He had grown so fast over the course of the school year that his pants no longer reached his shoes.

They went into Little Rock to shop at Blass's where his grandmother had once bought a dress. Timon found a tiger vest like the one worn by Maynard G.

Krebs. He begged and pleaded, but his mother refused to get it for him. Only when Timon cried so fervently that it embarrassed her in front of the store clerk did his mother relent. Timon laid the vest on top of his toy box and waited for Monday morning.

Before his arrival, his classmates had gotten together and realized that all their erasers were missing. They had reported the theft to the teacher by the time Timon showed up. She inspected everyone's desk and found that only Timon's eraser had not been stolen. The teacher marched Timon to the principal's office.

Timon remained steadfast in his denial and the principal spanked him with the paddle. Timon never cried. He was a brave tiger. When the punishment ended, he took a razor blade from his sock and, before anyone could stop him, sliced open his arm from wrist to elbow.

There was no saving the little boy. As he lay dying at the hospital, Timon tried to speak, but no one heard him. He wanted to make sure they buried him in the vest he was wearing and that on his headstone they wrote, "Here lies Timon—the Tiger Boy."

LITTLE BOY

I asked the little boy to show me how it is done;
how does one be nice, how friendly, how kind,
when no love comes from above
and only pain echoes the morning call for help?

It was you who deserved the attention, the praise.
You survived when others failed;
you kept your heart intact.

Show me the way through the mirror of life,
the maze of stones and sirens that sing
to distract me from the truth and give cause
for hope that all is well—when all is false.

Bring me back from that desire for death.

ONCE

Once a young pine spoke to me and said,
"Touch down between my branches and
let the sap stick to your hands."

Once the moon spoke to me and said,
"Raise your head.
Let me wash your face
with cream-colored light."

Once the sun spoke to me and said,
"You may dare to see Medusa's
face within my shine."

Once the dark-brown earth said,
"Smell the odor that will set you free."

Once the voice inside said,
"The story has been told and
the characters are content.
No one is troubled anymore."

And then I knew that I was dead.

STOOD A WOMAN

Stood a woman at the door he left
like the woman as he approached the hood
bereft of love,
the countenance of a paid whore.

She met him in the blood than runs
the street and counseled him
in the ways of easy death;
her seduction was oblivion's breath.

Stood the man before his mirror-self
his eyes were deep but not a child's;
his thoughts had never been
he was the progeny of ruin.

She mothered him as a bitch her pups
offering milk without touch
the men want to own his smell;
fathers use him as a crutch.

The end came as he expected
without notice or reprise;
the last thing he saw was
death in another's eyes.

DESPAIR

I am familiar with despair;
it comes when all is well
and all is not.

Despair greets my evenings after food
when a friend would offer praise.

When I raise my head from the sink
I am greeted by that stare.

When I am happy,
behind me is Time,
ready to wash me onto
the rocky bank of emotion, raw and bare.

In my loneliness I believe
I do not care.

I am familiar with despair.

BLANK DEATH

I am blank death,
an unfinished poem,
an artwork gone awry.

I am an epitaph,
a human joke,
a life shrunk dry.

I am nothing,
God's plaything,
a monkey cry.

I am a white bed,
a ruined being:
dead.

MRS. CALUMET'S WORKSPACE

One of Mrs. Calumet's coworkers recalled the segregation rallies in Little Rock. "You were part of that, weren't you, Mrs. Calumet?" the woman asked.

Several young boys were browsing the magazine rack nearby. They pricked up their ears at the question.

"That was a long time ago," Mrs. Calumet told her friend. "Jesse-Wyatt was the one who thought that way."

Jesse-Wyatt was Mrs. Calumet's husband. She knew when she met him that they held differences of opinion, but she was smitten with him during high school. Mr. and Mrs. Calumet came of age during the Great Depression, another topic the coworker, whose name was Eunice, liked to bring up as she looked for ways to pass the time. The two women spent many slow afternoons working the counter at the local variety store, which also served as a pharmacy in the small Arkansas town of Sibley.

Mrs. Calumet thought "Great Depression" was too dire a description for those times.

"We didn't care if a bank went under," she said to Eunice on one occasion. "We were doing good to have money stuffed in our mattresses!"

Eunice nodded. To the much-younger woman, Mrs. Calumet's assessment of the era sounded quaint.

"Our troubles out here in Sibley started when those greedy people moved in. They tricked folks into selling their mineral rights. Those Yankees knew there was money under people's farms, and they made a fortune. Then they moved away and left those old blue-hole bauxite pits."

Mrs. Calumet barely understood that bauxite was the source of aluminum, but she knew that the mines that sprang up around Sibley to extract the ore provided jobs at a time when the economy was at its worst.

Sibley was still rural in the mid-twentieth century, but it was close enough to Little Rock that people went there to shop for clothes and furniture. The Calumet family and Mrs. Calumet's folks, the Hollisters, wanted life in Sibley to remain unchanged. As long as they held onto enough land to grow vegetables and keep a few pigs and a milk cow, they were content. Mr. Calumet, Jesse-Wyatt, provided a good living as an electrician, but Mrs. Calumet didn't want to be a stay-at-home wife. They never had children, and she hated being alone. The job at the variety store gave her a chance to be around people.

Arithmetic had always come easy to Mrs. Calumet, even if she had done poorly in math during high school. That fact had more to do with her trying not to flaunt her intelligence than with any lack of mental ability. She wasn't pretty, and excelling academically wouldn't help her find a husband.

Mrs. Calumet was from a family who had lived in Sibley for so many generations that they'd forgotten when their ancestors arrived. She knew it was before the Civil War because stories about the conflict had been passed down to her, told to her by her aging grandfather. One story told how the family had dug a hiding place under the barn for her great-grandfather, Tom Hollister, a fugitive Confederate soldier. Tom hid in the dank space until 1865. Some stories said he didn't leave the hole for two years. But Mrs. Calumet's grandfather was born in 1864, and she couldn't imagine her grandmother sleeping with him in that cramped space. The sunken room still existed when Mrs. Calumet was a girl. But she only saw it once when her father tore down the dilapidated barn and filled in the hole with cement to prepare the foundation for a new structure.

Family legend had it that Tom Hollister never learned to read and that he managed the Hollister lands, situated about a mile from the Sibley line, by keeping the farm's accounting in this head. Mrs. Calumet believed that her skill with numbers came through her father. As a child, he told her that Hollisters never had to want because their "ability to figure" would save them in a pinch. Young Mrs. Calumet didn't know what he meant, but the idea stayed with her. It may have had something to do with the extreme care she gave to her accounts at home. She was able to keep the bills paid, no matter what the circumstances.

That knack for financial management caught the attention of the local pharmacist who ran the drug and variety store, when he was looking for a bookkeeper willing to work for low wages. Mr. Gooch had come south from Detroit as a young man during the bauxite era, hoping to profit from land speculation. But the lands he managed to acquire turned out to be worthless. Without the resources to return home, he courted and then married a local girl. He opened a shop to sell odds and ends on a parcel of land just off the main street. A mail-order certificate justified selling over-the-counter medicines, but soon he began selling prescription drugs. The drug company representatives didn't asked for credentials beyond his certificate. No one in Sibley questioned that "Doctor" Gooch was qualified. He knew the cure for almost every ailment, which saved many a doctor visit—something the moneyless residents of Sibley appreciated.

Mrs. Calumet caught the eye of Jesse-Wyatt during their senior year at Sibley High School. She benefited by a lack of competition. Many young people their age had dropped out of school to try to keep the family farm from going under. Even during the best of times, local girls married young. Most were taken by age sixteen. Bernice Calumet was an exception. She had not been courted by high school, and she worried about being too smart, if not pretty enough. Jesse-Wyatt had not shown much interest in girls, being more concerned with playing football and going out with his friends. But as those friends began to marry and leave school, he realized he better start looking. Bernice Calumet was pretty enough.

The Calumet family lived in one of the oldest houses in the area. They managed to keep the farm running even during the roughest part of the 1930s. Jesse-Wyatt and Bernice, to the envy of their neighbors, were able to honeymoon in

Eureka Springs. It was the farthest Mrs. Calumet would ever travel from Sibley. She never forgot the pleasant drive through the hills, their afternoon stop to hear bluegrass music at an outdoor festival in Mountain View, and the curiosity she felt when seeing the Queen Anne–style houses on the outskirts of Eureka Springs.

What she didn't allow herself to remember was the unpleasantness of that first night when her gentle-eyed Jesse-Wyatt thrust into her so hard that she almost couldn't refrain from calling out. Not knowing exactly what to expect from her first sexual experience, she thought it was normal—the burden of pain that befell women after being expelled from the Garden of Eden. Jesse-Wyatt didn't offer consolation or comfort. He didn't even kiss her afterward. He simply rolled onto his side with his back toward her and fell asleep.

The next night brought worse pain and even greater indifference from her husband. After they returned to Sibley, Jesse-Wyatt's attentions grew less frequent, as if he had lost interest in her. Mrs. Calumet didn't encourage him. After some time, though, Jesse-Wyatt found ways to excite himself. He began taking objects to bed that he used as probes. Mrs. Calumet concluded that sex was something to endure, and that a husband was someone to placate when necessary but to avoid otherwise. When her friends talked about their husbands, Mrs. Calumet reacted by pulling the collar of her blouse tight around her neck and stretching her skirt to cover her knees.

Mr. and Mrs. Calumet had been married for seventeen years when the incident involving Little Rock High School occurred. It was yet another aspect of her husband that she didn't understand.

Growing up, Mrs. Calumet's family had lived across the street from a family of "Negroes," the term she used growing up. Her mother had told her that the family had every right to be there. "Their grandpappies were the ones who worked the soil," she had said. "They got more right to be here than the white folk." It was a sentiment that went back to Tom Hollister.

The Calumets had owned slaves, and the tradition of Jesse-Wyatt's group was to "keep 'em in their place." The idea that black students would attend a white high school set Jesse-Wyatt's mind on fire.

On the day before the black students would begin classes, Jesse-Wyatt railed about it being the end of civilization. He preached racial purity and referred to black skin as "the mark of Cain." Mrs. Calumet tried not to listen.

The next morning Jesse-Wyatt jumped onto a flatbed truck with about a dozen other men heading to a protest in Little Rock. He had taken a shotgun from the rack in his pickup. Mrs. Calumet fretfully watched the evening news, as Jesse-Wyatt had not returned by nightfall. She felt some relief when nothing was said about violence or gunshots. Jesse-Wyatt came home around ten o'clock. Mrs. Calumet pretended to be asleep and was thankful that he didn't make any advances.

Mrs. Calumet enjoyed her job working for Mr. Gooch at Sibley Variety and Drug. During the early years, her desk was located at the end of the soda fountain in a space defined by cases of Coca-Cola, stacked to make a low wall. She was greeted by everyone who came into the store. When the soda jerk took a break or called in sick, Mrs. Calumet filled in for him. She thought it was great fun, an agreeable diversion from adding and subtracting columns of numbers.

By the late 1960s, the soda fountain wasn't making a profit. Mr. Gooch replaced it with a magazine rack. Later, shelves were added for albums when stereo systems became popular and people had money for such luxuries. Mrs. Calumet did her work at a table behind the counter in the back of the store. The space was cramped, but at least she had the chance to visit with customers from time to time.

As Sibley grew with the white flight from Little Rock, Mr. Gooch began to offer store credit. Mrs. Calumet needed a more secure place to work as she prepared customer statements to be mailed out each month.

When the dress shop next door went bankrupt (people in Sibley still sewed their own clothes from patterns, and the dress shop owner, having recently moved from Little Rock, didn't attract enough business from the newly arrived residents), Mr. Gooch acquired the space. He hired carpenters to break down the wall, join the two structures, and create an office for Mrs. Calumet. The best the carpenters were able to manage was a five- by eight-foot area at the end of a corridor. Mr. Gooch used the walls of the corridor to hold his stock of nonnarcotic drugs. He went to a local auction and bid on a desk small enough to fit Mrs. Calumet's workspace.

Mrs. Calumet didn't like it, but she would never think about complaining, much less quitting her job. As bad as it might be, the alternative was to sit at home and dread Jesse-Wyatt's return each evening. What she missed above all, being secluded in the isolated space, was the chance to visit with the customers. In the new surroundings, she had nothing to keep her occupied except the bookkeeping; the highlight of the day was reconciling the cash-register receipts with the money in the drawer. She prided herself on finding every discrepancy and never losing a single penny in her quest for precision.

The new workspace had a small opening for ventilation. If she stooped low enough while sitting at her desk, she could see into the store, which at least afforded her some sense that she wasn't completely alone. During the summer, she placed an oscillating fan in front of the opening. Since Mr. Gooch had not told the carpenters to allow vents along the corridor, the air didn't circulate otherwise. Some days Mrs. Calumet nearly fainted from the stagnant heat.

People in Sibley still remember Mrs. Calumet. They recall the events of her final day and refer to her with affection. The cause of the fire was never determined, but some people said that Mr. Gooch started it to collect insurance. Others said that a customer who couldn't pay a bill ignited the blaze, hoping to destroy the record of the debt.

The end came in the middle of August. Mrs. Calumet was struggling to find out why the cash drawer didn't match the receipts. She had narrowed the problem to a set of transactions in the afternoon of the previous day, when one of the local teenagers had been working at the register. Almost certainly, the girl had meant to hit the ten-dollar key but instead pressed the one reading one hundred dollars. The discrepancy was exactly ninety dollars. Mrs. Calumet felt a sense of victory in having discovered the problem, though it had taken her an hour to zip through the register roll and reach her conclusion.

When smoke started to billow from a vent in the ceiling over the drug counter, one of the customers yelled "Fire!" Everyone evacuated the store. Mrs.

Calumet might not have heard the alarm. The oscillating fan was noisy, muffling sounds from inside the store.

Unaware of the crisis, she fastened the register rolls with rubber bands. On the one where she'd found the problem, she wrote a note indicating the cause of the discrepancy. She put the rolls on top of the cash drawer and started toward the safe located near the exit of her workspace. That's when she recognized the danger.

Mrs. Calumet's body was found at her desk. The flames had never reached her workspace. The volunteer fireman who discovered her told Jesse-Wyatt that his wife died peacefully from smoke inhalation.

Eunice, who had become Mrs. Calumet's best friend, asked herself why Mrs. Calumet had not tried harder to escape.

Only Jesse-Wyatt could have figured that out.

RELATIONSHIP

THE ORIGIN OF THE COWBOY POEM

T he younger students at the university accepted Clancy as he was, even though at thirty-eight he felt embarrassed, not so much because of his age, but because he relied on student loans. Latifa worked with Clancy at the university library. Both were student assistants at the circulation desk. One evening Latifa invited Clancy to join her at a local pub called "Huey's." It was her birthday, and that's where she wanted to celebrate. Latifa struck a regal pose, positioning her large body on two carefully situated stools. She proudly began the evening with back-to-back Kamikazes, and still she spoke clearly and maintained her poise when getting up to shoot a game of pool. Friends whom Clancy also knew from the library, Jim, Shawn, Ty, and Michelle, became so drunk that they could barely point a cue stick. Clancy had one goal for the evening: to outlast these much-younger colleagues. He wasn't sure he could outlast Michelle, whom he'd witnessed finishing off a bottle of vodka with barely a misstep in her gait. Michelle admitted to being an "accomplished drinker."

Midnight, the finale of Latifa's birthday celebration, came with an order of White Russians for all. Having spent the last of her money on the gathering of friends, Latifa went home. So did Jim, Shawn, and Ty. Michelle remained. She flirted at the bar with a sexy man who looked like he could have been a member of the university football team. Clancy wouldn't know; he didn't care about sports. All he cared about was that Michelle would leave with the jock, and he would be jealous.

Huey's was very much a straight bar, and Clancy knew he'd better watch himself, but the alcohol made it hard for him not to stare at some of the handsome men seated around him. He feared his wandering eyes would get him beaten up and decided to leave before he lost control.

"Bye, Michelle," he said to his friend. Then, without thinking, he added, "I'm going to go find some dick."

"Good luck, honeybuns," Michelle said. The jock paid no attention to what Clancy had said. His eyes were focused on Michelle's ample bosom.

Clancy walked the half-mile to Panic! his favorite gay bar in Lincoln. Panic!—dive that it was—opened all manner of opportunities to his imagination. Country boys came into town intent on plying their trade, presumably because things weren't going well back home on the farm; at least that was Panic!'s supporting mythology. Clancy wondered if the gay boys from the Nebraska prairies weren't simply trying to find relief from the local expectations imposed on them of nothing but marriage, children, and a future of self-deception.

When Clancy entered the bar, taking his usual seat near the pinball machine, he noticed a young man playing pool with another fellow. This wasn't a farm boy, unless he was from a prison farm. Clancy was immediately attracted to the ruffian, finding his black felt hat and denim jeans sexy. His boots were well-worn, as if they'd endured a thousand miles of walking and traversed countless varieties of soil. The sleeves had been torn off the young man's black shirt. Tattoos of spider webs and animals on his arms were not rendered well. Clancy reckoned they had been drawn from memory by a cellmate in prison.

Despite the young man's look of destitution, the faux-cowboy's eyes were round and friendly. He smiled easily, camouflaging the pain that seemed to creep from the corners of his eyes.

"I'd like to buy a drink for the cowboy playing pool," Clancy told the bartender.

"He's drinking Coke. Is that all right?"

Clancy waved the bartender on his way, impressed that the good-looking pool player was a teetotaler. Delivering the drink, the bartender motioned toward Clancy. The cowboy sauntered over.

"Hey. Thanks, man."

Before Clancy could respond, the cowboy returned to the pool table. Every time he missed a shot, he came over to speak to Clancy. Clancy learned that the young man was on the street and that he needed money. Clancy smiled at the familiarity of the come-on and was amused by the speed with which "Cowboy" got to the point.

"Come with me. Let's fool around. I'll give you some cash."

"Thanks," the cowboy said, but not with much enthusiasm.

Clancy had surprised himself. He almost never approached anyone, especially when it was to offer cash for sex.

"I have to check on my Lab," the cowboy said as they went out the back door. The cowboy stooped to hug a Labrador retriever tied to a post. Clancy couldn't help notice the deep affection that the cowboy showed the dog and the enthusiasm the dog showed its master.

"My partner in there, the one playing pool with me, he'll watch the dog while I'm away."

"What's your name?" Clancy asked.

"Steve," the cowboy replied, but with a degree of hesitancy that made Clancy doubt that was the name on his driver's license.

"It's a short walk to where I live," Clancy said, hoping the cowboy wouldn't back out when he revealed the rest. "I live in a dorm."

Steve gave Clancy a long look. "How old are you?"

Clancy laughed nervously. "I'm as old as I look. I decided to go back to school after giving up on everything else." It was a well-rehearsed story. "I'm an anthropology student. My thesis is on nineteenth century free love movements."

The cowboy had already lost interest, so Clancy stopped talking, and they resumed their journey. Ten minutes later they were in Clancy's dorm room. The pair barely fit on the narrow bed. The cowboy didn't say much. He lay down and waited to see what Clancy wanted to do. When he realized what an easy trick it was going to be, he stretched out and put his hands behind his head.

Clancy took his time unbuttoning the black shirt and then peeling it off as the cowboy stretched out his arms to assist. Clancy opened the fly of the denim jeans and felt the radiating heat. Cowboy had more body hair than Clancy preferred, but it was silky and soft to the touch. Clancy pressed his cheek against the black underwear and felt an immediate response. He gazed toward the cowboy's face and made out several tattooed names, probably former loves, etched into his stomach and chest. They were jailhouse efforts, tattooed with Bible ink and a heated safety pin. Clancy conjectured that beneath whatever criminal behavior had sent him to jail, Steve was a man of passion who wanted to retain the experience of his loves by imbedding the names in his flesh.

Images of what the cowboy's life must have been like faded as Clancy lifted the cotton shorts and pulled them down to Steve's ankles. He turned off the lamp on the nightstand. Clancy suckled like a newborn calf with his head turned sideways on the cowboy's furry stomach.

"You've got another fifteen minutes," came Steve's dispassionate voice.

The situation had revealed itself for what it was: a transaction.

Steve rose from the bed, turned on the lamp, and dressed. Clancy gave Steve the paltry sum he had in his wallet. Steve left without another word.

Clancy turned on his computer, loaded a new document, and began to write.

COWBOY LOVE

The black dog, a puppy,
tongue like a Spam-burger,
"What a sweet dog."
Labrador retriever
in a dark alley, with only
his master to retrieve.

I am the master now,
who pays the price
for one hour's time.
The Lab must wait,
the tattooed master is mine,
in a tiny cell, on a narrow bed.

The black felt hat, Nebraskan symbol,
I remove it, and the master's hair is
jet-black and long.
I take off the shoes and gray socks,
and then the belt and the black jeans.
He's wearing black underwear.

Fluffy hair nests his manhood,
soft on my nose, mouth full of the taste
of him, my tongue cupped to savor arrested time.
And I nod to the mirror winking at me.

Cowboy has a sweet smile,
but I only saw it at the bar.
Now his eyes are closed, and his hands pillow
the back of his head; the long body stretches
out as a rental for my hour, for my tastes while
I work to swallow future generations.

"Fifteen minutes, and I have to leave."
Words invade the magic like a treble
clef on the printed page, and then I
realize I had turned off the light,
forgotten my rented time.

It's no good; I can only think of lonely
dogs and see the anxious eyes of lost love,
and I remember too much and, with the light,
it is the cold stare of price tag, and the
time is now to return real love,
to the cowboy and his Labrador.

AT THE BAR

It was an evening Lautrec would have drawn
had he made it past the vampires
and the loud museum yawn.

This was a night for the Empress,
not the queen.
She lip-synched to impress.

And there was Cowboy
sans Labrador—
this was his ploy:

The phone rang
and he ran as
Empress sang.

Back again, dollar down:
Remember to watch me play so I won't lose my ass.
Something tells me, boy, you seldom lose your ass.

COMPELLING LOVE

What a compelling emotion love is,
how debilitating and tragic,
what exhilaration, how heroic.

Did I step into your life by accident?
And did you stumble upon me unawares?
Or was a cosmic and vicious plan at work,
a trap laid to ensnare two hearts and cause
them, beating apart, to join as one.

Who knows where this will end—or if it will.
That is the nature of beginnings when the heart stirs,
when the swirl may lead to maelstrom or geyser.
Who knows? Not I and not you.

If a road lies ahead, no streetlamps guide the way.
Along the gutters run the vermin ready to snatch
up the detritus we leave behind—jolly, strolling together.
Shall we restaurant with wine, look deeply at each other?

What a compelling time,
what attraction, our minds conjoined,
our bodies entwined.
And then apart. One are two again.
So let me ask you—Do you know?
What comes in the wake of this?

FOR ANYONE WHO COULD BE A LOVER

No conclusion should be made.
What was said is not a work in stone,
to have all there is—that is a mighty leap.

I will not be done,
had in a moment's conquest—
but to the loving heart that
woos me with Romance and subtle embrace,
that heart will penetrate to the core of my being
and receive the soul's surrendered heat.

I will not be done:
No doer shall be my penetrator.
Only a kind word and a gentle kiss,
to him I will be made, not done.
Are you the one that woos me with Romance?

IMAGINARY TOM

Are you now imaginary Tom,
kept alive in one-sided e-mails,
given spirit by a longing that never arrives?

Will your image fade without a picture in my hand,
without the sound of your voice recorded
on the answering machine?

How can I let this die, the emotion that propelled us,
the compelling love that irresistibly made us say to each other
what we said.

That you were for me in that instant I have no doubt.
That I was made for a brief moment the object of your desire,
there was no mistaking.

Now are we imaginary friends, different in each other's thoughts,
I the burden you seek to discard,
you the lover I created from the mist of longing.

My imaginary Tom may never be dispelled by the flesh
and blood Tom at the other end, the silent side.
Imaginary Tom is alive and flourishes.

Can my imaginary self be in your heart too,
remain what you thought I was
and find a home there through timeless night?

MOTHER'S LOVE

Mother's love is like a rose.
When a thorn pricks the finger
the hurt is ignored at first.

Then a festering begins
and the small tip of the thorn
reminds you that it is still
buried deep inside.

Nothing can extract that kind of love
but a sharp needle, perhaps,
sterilized in the flame of the gas stove.

Mother's love is like a rose.

BEING

"A SUNDAY WHEN I WAS YOUNG"

Today is Sunday.
The paper says that Ted Hughes
wants us to know what he feels
about Sylvia Plath. He has written
a new book of poems about it.
But I don't care about what
Ted Hughes feels, one way or another.
I don't even know what I feel about myself.

One Sunday, I believed in God and went to church.
Then I found a different god and joined a cult.
Another Sunday I stopped believing in anything
beyond the flesh
—and that colors the way I feel about life.
I am living in a dead body;
I will never see the mix of another and me
in the face of a child.

Did my being gay cause me to journey
among the exotics of our culture?
Did my father's coldness urge me to seek
the affections of other men?
No answer will satisfy the ache of knowing
—this world has no place for me.

I wait for another Sunday.

CIRCUS MAXIMUS

Is this my circus maximus?
Is that a soul I see rising from your eyes?
The heart calls out in a small voice
and seeks an answer that will cover
each contingency, blend with love, cruelty,
and jokes, and smooth a path to the beginning
where heart gave birth to darkness
when the beacon dimmed.

A bomb exploded in my mind and scattered
my self like seeds to the ends of existence,
each sprouted and made a life,
made a life and grew, and some roots
touched the leaves that waved
with semaphore signals telling the wind their
relative position while others
brought water and food, and
a mind once divided, knitted to become
the self I am now.

I have been one to plumb his heart
seeking the depths you have,
but don't set course.
I bring back to you the findings and
brief you on what is there—we all
have the same heart,
we are from the one,
We hail from the same source.

CLOUDS

Some say this is the top of the world,
The disk-flat earth that stretches like
A quilt of soil and moss and roofs,
Fires that burn a hole through to Hades
Have no beginning and no end,
No top, no middle, no underside.

This is a new world, one you did
Not see the last time you died,
The last time you soared on air
Filled with the toil of past lives,
Anticipation of a new endeavor
With a new karmic load.

These are clouds that no one
Saw yesterday, that existed in
The mist not yet risen from the sea,
In the breath of carnate creatures
Not yet evolved like you and me.

And once I take in the view
It is gone with the life that
Just as briefly fled on the breeze
And brought me to the clouds.

HOMO DOMESTICUS

I believe in the almighty Power of Selection
That grew Lucy's lip and extended Adam's rib,
The power that gave rise to brute force
And tender love.

Time was that Adam's rib
Caught the dart and, wounded,
Lay dying at his brother's hand.
That was the band of Early Man.

And at the lake that Leakey found,
A tool was made that fed the bride,
No longer could our human nature hide.
Lips then touched
and the rib caged a heart that beat with jealousy
—but altruistic in equal measure.

We made a god in our image,
And selected what we would believe,
Relieved that a force had made the world,
While the heavens rained with fire and ice.

At home, then, in this world,
Selected for the hearth and home,
Homo domesticus, like the tamed
Creature in a zoo, forgot he was a wild brute
—once with protruding jaw.

The awe faded and examination, that science,
Made our thoughts supreme.
Homo domesticus is what he seems,
In the end no less, and no more
Than he deems.

I WISH THERE
WERE ∧ GOD

I wish there were a god,
Something I could truly
Fire with cosmic blame—instead this rage
Is laid at the feet of a hominid father
Intoxicated by a conscious thought.

If only this flesh did not scream the pain
And if this mind did not know the meaning
Of the words it spoke;
If only death could be the absolute end
Instead of a quantum joining with cosmic minds
Writhing in the dark-matter vacuum.

Then perhaps I could live this out,
Portray the hopes that seep through
No matter how the weight is brought to bear
Somewhere—out there—beyond this cranial mass
Someone or something must be brought to task.

This is all I ask, we, those cursed with thoughts,
Aware that we are not the god and will not die,
And will not know the love we think is there;
We ask for oblivion—and get it not
We ask for answers and meet the void.
We don't even think that's odd.

In truth,
I wish there were a god.

MAHLER'S NINTH

Ruminations, ruffians, rapacious
Rastafarians.
These words ascend to present thoughts,
Present a contrast
An insight or perhaps a
Glimpse of your spirit in the air.

Something demands
I share the words,
Put on paper random thoughts
I ought not to ponder, but prepare;
Tonight I hear the Ninth of Mahler,

Knowing a Tenth began, that
No amount of rumination
No ruffian, no matter how
Rapacious, no Rastafarian,
Not even I, even in trance,
Shall ever complete.

MISSING THE MARK

How perverse religion can be.
My tears of repentance missed the mark
Not touching upon the dark space
Where childhood lay,
But serving the wrong god
In another place.

Those tears should be the balm
That heals my soul,
Not currency that feeds ego's coffers
To build temples of vainglorious power—
This is now my time, and my own hour.

I have known gods in my past,
And loved the angels who rebelled,
Followed their rituals and lost myself in ruinous life,
Saved not through religion's chants or meditation's bell
But through quenching pain with a tearing balm,
Entertaining questions that, finally, I dared to ask.

MY GOD

My god is animal,
he enjoys sex
and watching a good fight,
he enters little boys at puberty
and masquerades as woman,
he watches reality dim
as death approaches—
then escapes.

RESURRECTION

There is resurrection from the dead:
Although my heart was laid to rest at seven,
Insisting not to live, there began a pretended life.

The day was foretold by words, corpuscularian,
Sealed in deep folds of memory, outside my daily life.

Those words took form in the ephemeral breath of friends
That sent them, virtually said, through the air into my head:
There is resurrection from the dead.

A life regained grows again in the murky soil of life,
Nurtured by attention to the unread heart,
The hero whose blood returned and warmed
The young boy laid on his bed, yes,
There is resurrection from the dead.

THE GOD YOU WERE

Facing you was almost a religious thing
Wondering if you were indeed God
Or merely the DNA spark from a mother's womb.

In the end, the god I thought you were
Turned out to be nothing but an odd king
Holding court in a lower realm.

My heart recognized your diminished state
Admitting that you indeed did die,
Expiring such a long time ago.

And now, it is the dim echo of your voice
I hear fading into the past,
A former life that will stay with me forever.

What came before will not be the design
of the future I now anticipate,
Encouraged by hope and expectation.

I know that I shall succeed in spite of you,
We both having now attained the life
And yes, the death, that is rightfully our due.

REFLECTION

WALTER'S LAST NIGHT

anic! was one of two gay hangouts in Lincoln, Nebraska. It was a dimly lit bar that smelled of rodent piss, with barstools that danced on uneven legs and made the patrons wonder if they were drunker than they thought. Men who frequented the place rarely went home alone.

Walter Pendergast, an assistant professor, showed up at the bar every night just before eleven o'clock. The bartender knew his schedule and had his glass of Bud Light waiting for him. During his first hour at the bar, Walter told himself that he would finish his beer, maybe have one more, and then go home. But it never worked out that way. After his third glass, the interval between drinks shortened to ten minutes. Invariably he would order a pitcher. By the time he poured the last dregs of foam, the bar was sticky with spilt beer. Chance the bartender kept his patience because Walter tipped well, unlike the other professors who came to the bar.

By the time he moved on to gin and tonic, Walter had forgotten all about getting home early to prepare the next day's assignments. After all, he told himself, he'd taught his classes the same way for three years, and no one in authority had said a thing. What did he care if a black market for answers to his exams thrived in the dormitories? His annual reviews praised the fact that his students performed well.

Walter soon tired of gin and switched to Jack and Coke and, before long, would switch again, to Jack straight up. Now he wanted to find adventure, something to counteract the doldrums of everyday existence. His mediocre talents doomed him to teaching college freshmen the basics of computer programming. He could think of no profession less rewarding for a man who fancied himself a master of combinatorics.

Though he hardly admitted it to himself, Walter drank to assuage a feeling of guilt. The stalwart ROTC boys who came directly to his class from drill practice, pheromones bursting from their armpits, made him dizzy with desire. Then there were those on the other end of the spectrum: the students who dressed in the grunge style of the day. They had a different allure, but it was no less erotic. They met his eyes dead-on. Did they know what was on Walter's mind and find it amusing, enticing even? Walter believed so.

Some of the ROTC recruits came to Panic! but Walter dared not approach them. He wasn't sure if they were gay or if they just liked the pool table, the one thing the bar had going for it. The table was tournament-sized and fairly new. Most importantly, the management ignored gambling. But even if Walter discovered that one of them was gay, he wouldn't make a move. Walter was not handsome in any classic sense. He wore heavy glasses, and his belly pressed hard against the front of his shirt. No matter how much he dieted during the day, the evening bouts of drinking counteracted the effort.

Around the time he ordered his first Jack and Coke, Walter noticed a particularly handsome group of young men entering the bar. He knew they weren't students because they wore actual thrift-shop clothes, not the grunge attire that was designed to look secondhand. The uneven way these new fellows tucked in their shirts, and the calculated manner in which their jeans were unzipped a quarter of the way down their flies also gave them away. Walter knew they had come to town hoping to supplement their farmhand salaries. On another level, they sought relief from the boredom of small-town life.

The week had not gone well for Walter in his efforts to seek companionship. The one evening he left the bar with a young man, the fellow hopped out at a stoplight, having seen a female hooker that he knew. Walter parked along the side of the road, hoping the guy would return, but when a police car circled the block and slowed down beside him, Walter drove on. He returned to the bar and got so drunk that he didn't remember getting home. The next few nights, he walked to Panic! The university would frown on a professor getting a drunk-driving charge, and Walter didn't want to take any chances.

The bar thinned out around one o'clock in the morning as the farm boys paired up with older men. Walter had braced himself for another night of loneliness when a fellow dressed in a black cowboy hat took the barstool beside him.

"What's up, bud?" the fellow said in a gravelly voice.

Walter sized him up in a glance, noticing the faded blue jeans that had a strategic tear near the crotch.

"Hey, what're you looking at?" the fellow said with a sly grin.

"Just wondering where you bought your underwear. I'd like a pair of black briefs like that."

The fellow let out a guttural laugh as he took a bag of Bugler tobacco from his shirt pocket and rolled a cigarette. After letting a billow of raw smoke pass through his nostrils, he pointed his chin downward and said, "You can have this pair. I need the cash."

"What's your name?" Walter asked.

"I go by Ray," the young man said, and he reached under the bar and placed his hand on Walter's knee. Walter put his hand on top of Ray's.

"How did your hand get so rough?" Walter asked, grasping Ray's hand and rubbing the palm.

"Riding broncos," Ray said, smiling broadly.

Walter smiled at the sense of pride in his voice.

"I've broken horses since I was a kid. Got paid last Friday, but I spent it all. Goes fast, doesn't it?"

Walter nodded, "Sure does."

"You got hands like a woman," Ray observed as he reversed the position of their hands.

"I'm no woman," Walter protested. He hoped to signal what type of trick he would be were they to leave the bar together.

Ray considered how he might turn the conversation to his advantage. "I'm bisexual," he proclaimed.

"Well, being on the giving end helps you know what to do when you are receiving," Walter regretted sounding so professorial. He knew it wasn't a sexy attribute.

Cigarette smoke streamed from Ray's nostrils as he laughed at Walter's comment. "You got that right," he said.

Ray nodded toward the pool table. An ROTC boy had just leaned over the edge and was positioning himself for a difficult shot. "What do you think of that? I know what I'd do with those sweet cheeks."

"I wouldn't throw him out of bed," Walter confessed.

Ray found his opening. "Would you throw me out of bed?"

"Depends," Walter replied.

Ray took Walter's hand and placed it farther up his leg, "Want to go for a ride?"

"My car's parked at the university," Walter said. "I walked to the bar."

"That's OK. I have a car outside," Ray said, feeling for a moment better off than the professor he had landed. "Do you want to get some drugs and go party…that is, if you have the money?"

Walter looked askance at Ray. "You know exactly how much I've got. I saw you staring at my wallet when I paid for the drinks." Walter paused to read Ray's expression, hoping he hadn't put him off.

Ray didn't flinch.

"I'll put in twenty bucks for the drugs, and forty for, you know," Walter stammered. "I need the rest until payday."

Ray joined Walter in a round of schnapps, compliments of the bartender. While still feeling the quick surge of alcohol, they went outside to Ray's battered station wagon. Sacks of clothes and cardboard boxes that were bent at the seams filled it nearly to the roof.

"My old lady threw me out the other day," Ray explained. "Sorry about the junk. I'll make some room." He pushed a pillowcase full of laundry into the narrow space remaining above the boxes in the backseat.

Walter squeezed in, making sure to avoid the springs popping through the seat cushion.

"Not very comfortable, but it gets me where I want to go."

"And where's that?" Walter asked. He tried not to sound sarcastic, but he was having second thoughts about his decision to go on this ride.

Ray didn't hear Walter's question. "What are you into, man? Do you like speed? Do you smoke rock?"

"Let's smoke some rock," Walter said, surprising himself. He had done drugs during his senior year in college, but nothing since leaving rehab after he was fired from his first teaching position. With Walter's chubby face and dimpled chin, no one suspected him of having a dark side; no one thought him capable of breaking into a church and stealing the collection money, much less trying to sell a stolen car. But those were the circumstances that led to his dismissal. Incarceration or rehab were the choices given to him by the judge.

Ray backed out of the dimly lit parking lot and headed toward one of Lincoln's poorer neighborhoods. As they drove down Main Street near the university, Walter slumped in his seat. He dared not risk being seen. More than one policeman had made their reputation by catching a university professor in a compromising situation.

Ray slowed beside a phone booth in the parking lot of a Kwik Mart convenience store. An elderly man with dreadlocks approached the driver's side of the car.

"Hey, George," Ray called out, acknowledging the man. "Have you got it going on?"

The old man glared through the window at Walter.

"He's cool," Ray said.

George didn't look convinced. Still, he decided to chance a sale. "We need to go down the street," he said.

Walter squeezed in tighter to make room for George, who half sat on his lap, his knots of hair falling across Walter's shoulder.

"It's not far," George said, pointing the way.

They arrived at an apartment complex constructed of cinder-block walls painted white. Broken screens hung from the window frames. The intensity of the streetlights made Walter worry again about being spotted.

George got out first and went to the door of a ground-floor apartment.

"He'll be right back," Ray said, "Get your money ready."

"You should put in some of your own," Walter said. "I saw what was in your wallet, too, you know."

"Smart man," Ray growled.

Walter wished they could forget about the drugs and go to his place. He tried to suggest it, but Ray was coy. Ten minutes passed, then twenty, and Walter grew increasingly anxious. "I've heard bad things about this neighborhood," he said. "We should go."

Ray didn't argue the point. He had noticed a police car passing a few streets behind them as he watched in the side mirror. Ray started the car and drove away.

"I know another place." Ray said, but they only got speed. Does that work for you?"

"Sure. Why not?" Walter said, willing to agree to anything just to get going.

Ray drove to another group of apartments. These were older buildings with redbrick façades. Ray pulled into an alley and parked. Walter was prepared to walk away and find a route back to the main street.

"Two guys and a girl live upstairs," Ray said, holding Walter's arm. "I've known them a long time. They don't sell, but they might let us do some crystal with them."

"What about you and me?" Walter asked. He didn't want the drugs; he wanted Ray. He would agree only if the prospect of sex remained.

Ray grinned. "Maybe we can get a five-way going."

Walter hoped that Ray was joking. The one time Walter had done it in a group, everyone seemed to have a good time but him.

"What do you say?" Ray pressed, grabbing Walter's arm a little tighter.

Walter noticed the bulge in Ray's underwear; it was showing through the tear in his jeans.

Ray led Walter up a flight of stairs and knocked on an apartment door. Soon Walter heard a chain scraping against the doorjamb. The fellow who answered recognized Ray, but he didn't welcome them inside.

"It's OK," Ray said. "This is my homeboy."

The guy, who didn't seem to need much convincing, opened the door wide. Ray and Walter entered a room filled with stale air. A tied-dyed sheet provided some gaiety to the otherwise drab decor. A VCR balanced precariously on top of an old television. Rows of tapes lined the shelves of a do-it-yourself bookcase. Walter noticed the pornographic titles, but couldn't make out if they were straight or gay.

A young man with a soft face and long black hair sprawled on the couch, partially covered by a crocheted throw. His beard was so faint that Walter wondered if he had yet begun to shave. The young man raised his hand as Walter passed. "I'm Kevin," he said in a quiet voice.

Walter took the boy's hand, but the weak grip put him off, and he quickly let go. Walter noticed that Kevin's eyes were shot through with a web of red veins and that track marks dotted his forearm.

An emaciated girl with dirty-blond hair emerged from the bedroom carrying a shoe box. She wore a black tank top with jeans cut so short that they exposed the fringed edge of her panties. She took a seat on the floor beside the coffee table and began sorting through the contents of the box, putting safety pins in one pile and bobby pins in another. Walter had heard in rehab about the behavior of meth addicts; they tended to fixate on pointless activities.

The guy whom Ray had come to see was in the bedroom looking at himself in a hand mirror and running a finger under the brown hair around the contours of his face.

"I'm Bobby," the guy said, putting the mirror face down on the bedspread and extending his square hand to Walter.

Bobby was built like a squat football player. Walter felt drawn into his fathomless dark eyes that managed to retain a sparkle despite the obvious dissipation. Bobby opened a drawer and took out three syringes. But Walter drew the line at shooting up; he didn't even like to watch people stick needles in their arms.

Bobby tightened a rubber hose around his arm and pulled the end with his teeth. He thumped a vein until he got a response and then expertly slid the needle under his skin and drew blood until it mixed when the drug. Then he shoved the concoction back into his body. His teeth lost their grip on the hose and it fell away. Bobby's next act was to run to the window and peer through the curtains, which was a marked sign of extreme paranoia.

Ray could tell by Walter's expression that he didn't shoot up. He took a container of white powder from the dresser and laid out a line for Walter to snort, using the hand mirror that Bobby had laid on the bed. Ray fashioned a makeshift straw from a pen. Walter anxiously inhaled the drug, but he withdrew at the stinging sensation.

"This is why I prefer coke," Walter said, pressing his index fingers on either side of his nose, hoping to relieve the pain.

Ray took Walter into the bathroom and shut the door. "Inhale some water," he said. "That'll dilute it."

Walter did as he was told. The water helped, but it also made him dizzy.

They heard a soft knock on the door. "It's Kevin. Come on, guys; I'm dying out here."

Ray opened the door, but instead of guiding Walter out of the bathroom, he admitted Kevin, who wore only an old pair of jeans. Walter succumbed to his own fixation—on Kevin's beadlike nipples.

"What's going on in here?" Kevin asked. "Are you guys done or what?"

"It's hard to pee when you're high on speed," Walter said, turning to the urinal and unzipping his pants.

Kevin, unwilling to wait, snapped open the top button on his jeans and joined Walter at the bowl. Walter watched intently as Kevin released a powerful stream.

"That's what I thought you guys were into," Kevin said as Walter maneuvered behind him and reached around to help him aim.

Ray seemed content that Walter had made a move on Kevin. He placed his syringe on the edge of the sink and prepared a fix. Walter watched as the needle went into Ray's skin, noticing how Ray's eyes rolled upward. Ray collapsed, sitting down in what seemed like slow motion and leaving the syringe half full.

Kevin pulled away from Walter and took the syringe from Ray's arm to stick it into his own. "No use letting good drugs go to waste," he said.

Right at that moment, Walter spotted a trail of blood streaming under the bathroom door. His heart beat furiously as he followed the stream. A bloody hand fell from the chair in Bobby's bedroom as Walter entered. A ghastly puddle had formed. Walter forced himself to take the last few steps forward. Bobby's neck had been slashed, exposing white bone and gristle. Walter glanced around the room, fearing for his own life.

The girl! Walter had not even learned her name. He would barely be able to describe her to the authorities.

Shrill sirens pierced the air. Floodlights shot across the walls. Red and blue flashes of brilliant light attacked Walter's eyes from beyond the curtains. He would be the one to answer the brutal pounding at the door, to gaze into the fierce eyes of the nightmare, and to see, forever, nothing else.

ON A DAY LONG AGO

The world had a definition—
that was about 1960.
The borders blurred with Kennedy,
permeated by the San Francisco poets,
and shattered by Oswald's gun.

I was born around that time,
and still recall the borders.
Father railed that a negro attended
my first-grade class
but his anger subsided when the boy
turned out to be Hawaiian.

Symbol of a changing world—
that was Little Rock Arkansas
where three years earlier
that same father led alumni
with guns outside the high school:
"There go the damn niggers."

And when it turned out I was gay,
the borders fenced me in.
Some borders take longer than others
to collapse; some take longer to give in
to reality, standing against what others want.

My hero was Maynard G. Krebs.
When I watched Dobie Gillis, I related
to the future Gilligan,
the misfit, the good guy
who doesn't understand why people see him that way.

He only wants to be liked—to say the border
should be taken down and cease to exist—
to be what we are; but always, there is a law
that strains our progress.
Marriage straight, marriage gay,
and tell me, is this another day?

GROW UP

Did I not grow up?
I don't remember.
The house is mute;
the soil has been replaced.

Once I looked at myself
and saw the mirror reflecting
not me, but eyes fading.
Is that not me growing up?

I had a dog whose bones
rest for an archeologist to read
beside the rust from my
hamster-coffin lunch box;
I have a memory half-formed.
I am no good, he said, the voice
that now belongs to no body.

I ask again, did I not grow up?
Images stain the accretion of paint.

A primitive speaks
through colors and cloths
layered against the day; I ask again.

The answer is not one I want.
I did not recover the lost memory
nor dispel the false emotions
of haunted nights.
Only the voice that will not die remains.

WHEN I WAS SEVEN

I died when I was seven
And since then lived a pretended life.
There are pins stuck in the map of living
To guide me back along the way,
Each a word that self-made sorcerers use
To ward off pain.

Wasn't there promise in youth?
Remind me, isn't there a door on which to knock?
It is the end of Truth, the end of Time,
And the demon at the gate knows I am arrived.

Behind him, beaten down, locked in a mental realm
Inaccessible but to the few who mountains climb
To love the view, a boy hides with eyes wide shut against
The angry fist. He listens and waits for the gods to call.

Rescuer of a soul that can't exist and must be made
Of murderous rage and hate for the demon of the mind
The torturer of the soul—he must die and die with pain.

Not this time, you say, but again as in the past
This determined boy will last beyond the dark,
Beyond the heart that cries and is lost,
To see what lies in the life that is pretended,
Made real for the betrothed intended.
Call from the dark and wake to Now.

Imbue a determined will to find what is there
Beyond the cruel warmonger
Beneath the bedding of disgrace and shame.
Call to him and make the claim.

It is the end of Truth, the end of Time.
Harsh eyes of the evil kind peer back
And I stop his heart dead cold.
No longer live with what is old
But find the door is opened
And the demon faced.
The final destination
Starts anew.

CRYING

If I sat crying,
missing the loss of love,
would you be the one to comfort me?
With a kiss upon the brow,
would you take my hands and say,
"I am for you, we are together now"?

MIST

Is that mist arising from the valley part of me?
Can the smoke drifting up from the farmer's chimney
be from food cooked to ease my soul?
This place—was it given so I might be at home?
Will that Pinnacle Mountain whose peak was once
a vantage point for youth call me now
and let me trek beyond the valley of the mist
and dispel the sorrow into which my life descended?

NEW ROADS

I am on new roads now,
not made by myth pressed
down by naked feet.

I followed that messiah before.
He is not in front to guide me now.
The way that holy cartographer pointed
was toward darkness.

I found no true prophet there.

I am on new roads now,
not made by myth pressed
down by naked feet.

No cartographer has presaged the route.
All maps are my own.
I follow old ways that are new to me.

In a short life I have seen much through others' eyes.
Mine are not like the eyes of crocodiles

that see clearly with three folds
protecting from the murky waters.

That animal trinity does not protect me
when I see clearly
who I am and where I must go.

My road is sunk in the mire of being human
as I follow it alone.
I sense the destination;
It is a place where others wait for me.

I am on new roads now,
not made by myth pressed
down by naked feet.

TO A THERAPIST,
FOR A CHILD

Don't call attention to the presence.
Let it cry, exposed for all the world
…this is me…you see.

This is no personification, no incarnated child.
Let him hide in full view,
sobbing for all that never was
and cannot be, for
…this is me…you see.

Let the floodgate open and the torrent flow,
for in this way we gather in the storm,
embraced against the sea,
hiding in plain sight as the kraken wails.
There is much to tell of this life against the norm,
for sitting here now, you see,
…this is me.

VALÉRY'S RIDE

Valéry's nieces and nephews called him their "bachelor uncle," and his aunts and uncles were quick to remind him that time was running out if he wanted to have a family of his own. Valéry didn't think his family knew he was gay, even though he knew he measured up to the stereotypes. He never dated, only had male friends, and after attending college, moved back home to live with his mother.

It wasn't as though Valéry had much to keep secret. His only love affair had been during his college days, and that was nearly a quarter century ago. He had gay friends in New Orleans, but he never went out to bars and almost never came home later than nine in the evening. Valéry was content to live with his mother, Louisa, in the Garden District house his family had owned for generations. Everyone admired Valéry's devotion to his mother and dedication to the upkeep of the property. They respected Valéry, even if they didn't understand his remaining single.

When Valéry's employer offered him a position in Baton Rouge, it was an easy decision. He longed to be alone, away from the family pressures and the endless advice on how to find a wife. Louisa had tried to talk him out of leaving, but Valéry had also started to fear that time was running out for him. He was tired of not having a confidant, someone who knew him completely. He was tired of sleeping alone.

Valéry found a small house on the edge of Baton Rouge and refurnished it to his liking. No more dusty antiques and the clutter of knickknacks. Louisa became more agreeable when she realized that Valéry would see her at least once a week. Each Sunday, he took his mother to Mass, and he never missed a funeral. Funerals were a time to celebrate. The last time he had gotten drunk was during the festivities after his uncle César died. His cousins put the casket on rollers and hauled it inside each bar his uncle had frequented when he was alive. A trombone-and-drum band followed them, playing such authentic ragtime it seemed as though time had stopped.

When news came that Hurricane Katrina was bearing down on the coast, relatives flocked to the ancestral home, which was on high ground in the Garden District. Valéry sighed with relief when Louisa called to say that everyone was safe. She ended her call saying, "The family needs you, Valéry."

Then Hurricane Rita struck land. Biloxi bore the brunt of the damage. Within a day of the storm, cousins began to show up in Baton Rouge. Many arrived on flatbed trucks, reminiscent of refugees fleeing a war zone. Valéry opened his small home to the relatives, making room by allowing them to put down sleeping bags wherever they could find a few feet of floor space. The house became so packed, the air became hard to breath. It didn't help that the toilet backed up and finally overflowed. Valéry dug a latrine in the backyard and pitched a camping tent over the trench. It would have to do until the city found a way to accommodate the crush of people escaping even worse misery along the coast.

Relatives of Valéry's friend, Ferdinand—who went by Fern—arrived in Baton Rouge on a FEMA bus. Fern's kin had gotten to dry land by making a raft from the broken planks that had been their house and using poles to guide it. Fern hoped that Valéry might have an extra room and showed up at his front door to ask in person. When he saw the patchwork of bedding on the living room floor, he realized that Valéry was dealing with a catastrophe of his own.

"Miss Thing," Fern said when Valéry came to the screen door. "Look at us! We've become Mother Teresa. I hope they canonize us for giving up our homes like this."

Valéry looked behind him, worried that someone might have heard his friend's language. Valéry might camp it up when visiting Fern's home, but never in public, and never in front of family.

"Fern!" Valéry protested. "No girl talk, all right?"

Fern sighed a long sigh and pursed his lips. "Girlfriend, if your family isn't going to accept you after all you're doing, then so much for them."

"Please!" Valéry insisted.

Fern looked past Valéry into the front room. "They're all asleep in there, anyway. Not a creature stirring, not even a mouse."

"I'm afraid the boys would eat a mouse stupid enough to show its whiskers around here," Valéry laughed. "There isn't much to eat. No one has any money."

Valéry wasn't sure how much more he could endure. It seemed there was no escape from being the dependable member of the family, the one who was always there to help. It was a role that made him feel needed, but not fulfilled. Fern had talked of sainthood, but Valéry was no Mother Teresa. He wanted his freedom.

Valéry's dilemma reached a turning point when his employer, happy about the way he had brought order to the Baton Rouge office, offered him an assignment in Reston, Virginia. Valéry wanted to take the job, but felt guilty about the prospect of abandoning those depending on his generosity. He had a long talk with his great-aunt Palmyra, who had been among the last to arrive from New Orleans. Valéry explained that going to the east coast was a great opportunity that would enhance his career. Palmyra agreed to take responsibility for the situation in Baton Rouge.

A stout woman in her eighties, Palmyra was the family matriarch. "Do what you must in order to survive in this old world," she counseled. "And don't worry about Louisa. I'll do the explaining to her. I'll send your Uncle Jacques if she needs help." Uncle Jacques was almost ninety, but had the build of a man in his sixties. He had even led the troop that carried César's casket to the bars.

Palmyra had great powers of persuasion, and Valéry knew that she would take care of Louisa and the rest of the family. Valéry decided to leave his car behind, and, as a last gesture of goodwill, quitclaimed the deed to the Baton Rouge property to Palmyra. When the time came for him to leave, Palmyra drove Valéry to the Greyhound Bus terminal. The thick predawn fog made it difficult to see the road, and they almost arrived too late. His employer had arranged for lodging upon Valéry's arrival in Virginia, but had not offered a stipend for travel. A bus ticket was all Valéry could afford, since the recent events had depleted his savings. Just before Valéry boarded, Palmyra took him aside and pressed a Dixie into his hand. Since he was a boy, Palmyra had insisted on referring to the ten-dollar bill by the term that gave the South its nickname.

"You have a glass of Sazerac on me once you settle in," she said. "Are you hearing me, mon cher?"

"Aunt Palmyra," Valéry said, gently refusing the money, "they won't have Sazerac where I'm going. You need this money more than I do."

Palmyra's eyebrows rose nearly to her hair line. "They have no Sazerac, then I send you a thermos!" She laughed at the thought. "You need Sazerac, or no you sleep at night."

Valéry marveled at how his Aunt Palmyra never learned to speak proper English. Her French, though, was perfect, whereas Valéry's command of that language, even in Cajun dialect, left much room for improvement. He kissed his aunt on the cheek and boarded the bus. He knew he would miss having Sazerac and secretly hoped Palmyra would send him her private recipe of brandy, bitters, and sugar, mixed in proportions she had never shared with anyone.

As the bus crossed the boundary of the city and entered the sprawling countryside, Valéry had never felt so unconstrained by family expectations. If he found a lover, he would not have to worry about anyone seeing them together. He would be far from the suspicious eyes of conservative kin and the watchful gaze of Louisa. He imagined the new life awaiting him and the prospect of having a comfortable home and sharing it with a partner. He fell asleep, content in thoughts of endless possibilities. A ringing phone intruded. Valéry rushed to catch the call, not wanting to explain to Louisa about the man who always seemed to be visiting. A sigh passed Valéry's lips as he awoke from the dream, leaned his head against the window, and watched the scenery glide past.

Valéry did well in his new job. His salary allowed him to send money back home and still have plenty to put into savings. However, socially, he still had not found what he wanted. The real nightlife was in DC, not in the suburbs of Virginia, but the company had arranged a six-month lease on the townhouse in Reston, and it would have cost too much to break it. The saccharine neighborhood made him long for the moldy walls of his old home in New Orleans. He missed the oleander consuming the wrought-iron arch that led out to the cobblestone sidewalk, and the wisteria wrapping around the spiked-iron fence that surrounded the garden.

Valéry received frequent updates about the fate of his relatives. Palmyra had rallied to the cause, practically beating down the door of the local FEMA office until her demands for assistance were answered. Ironically, without the gainfully employed Valéry on the premises, Palmyra had a stronger case for emergency aid. The family-member refugees began moving into FEMA trailers. Some went to live with other relatives whom Palmyra bullied for help.

Palmyra offered the house back to Valéry when everyone had moved on, but he reminded her that she was the one whose home had been destroyed. He told her that she should remain in Baton Rouge as the focal point of communication with the far-flung clan. Palmyra feared that her beloved neighborhood would never be rebuilt. Perhaps the gambling interests would salvage the area and turn it into a decadent playground. They'd get their sinful hands on the Ninth Ward if they had the chance, and God knows what they would turn that into. So much for the genuine culture of Dixieland.

At the end of six months, Valéry scanned the "Living in Style" section of the *Washington Blade*, a gay-community newspaper, and decided to look for an apartment in Takoma Park, a small city in Maryland just over the DC border. Within a week, he had located a one-bedroom apartment up a flight of stairs, in a building near the Metro station. The manager was a friendly old gentleman who confirmed Valéry's one requirement—that he could have a dog. Valéry's colleagues at work had mentioned how they wouldn't have met anyone in their neighborhoods if they didn't have a dog. Valéry had not owned a dog since his bichon frise, Pimpernel, died when he was a teenager. After Valéry's father passed away, Louisa would not allow animals in the house.

Strolling through the Takoma Park farmers' market one Sunday morning, a few weeks after moving in, Valéry spotted a humane-society van with a sign advertising dogs rescued from the areas struck by Katrina and Rita. Valéry spent time with each dog in the mobile kennel. He finally chose a large canine that appeared to be a mixture of Labrador and collie, long-haired and gangly with an amiable personality. The dog took to him instantly, as if sensing a kindred spirit. He named him Luchen, a play on the French word for dog, "le chien."

On one of his first outings with Luchen, Valéry discovered a building that took up nearly a city block. A large sign stated that the Washington National Opera rehearsed upstairs. He saw men entering the building who he assumed were singers. A much smaller sign advertised an art gallery. Valéry pulled Luchen's leash tight and ventured into the lobby. When his eyes adjusted, he noticed large abstract paintings on the walls through a set of doors. A young lady sat on a folding chair next to a much older woman. They rose when Valéry and Luchen came into the gallery. The younger woman introduced herself and mentioned that she was the artist.

"Your dog is so unusual," the artist said. "What's his name?" She reached down to scratch Luchen's ear, but he turned on his back and wiggled, hoping instead to get his stomach scratched. "What's your name little fellow?"

"I call him Luchen," Valéry said.

The older woman laughed. "I know your accent. You must be from New Orleans."

Valéry nodded. He recognized her dialect as well, and almost ventured to guess the ward where she had grown up.

"Oh, I get it now," the girl said. "Le chien." She rubbed the dog's stomach and said, "I'm Doramae Cantrelle. This is my grandmamma, Marietta Cantrelle. We came from New Orleans after the levees broke."

Luchen whined when Doramae withdrew her attentions. Valéry pulled on the leash to make him stand, and then gave the one command that Luchen understood: "Sit."

"The house we lived in fell apart around us," Doramae explained. "The glass in the windows shattered. Grandmamma and I took refuge in the closet under the stairway. When the winds died down, we clung to the banisters for two days before rescuers arrived in boats; the entire first floor had flooded by then." She looked wanly at Luchen. "We never saw my dog, Missy, again, or Puss. We heard our tabby cat crying during the storm. We never saw any sign of her later on. Dogs find a way to survive, don't they, Luchen?" she said, patting the dog on his snout. "I doubt that Puss made it through. Cats hate the water so."

Valéry walked through the gallery and inspected Doramae's paintings; they were masterful works with swirls of vivid color that brought to mind the violence of the hurricanes.

"I'm no expert," Valéry said, "but I find your paintings evocative. I'm glad I stumbled onto this place."

"It's my last day," Doramae said.

"You mean for the exhibit?"

"And for our stay in this area. Grandmamma and I leave for Philadelphia tomorrow to live with our cousins who've found jobs there."

Valéry had met two gay couples since moving to Takoma Park. One pair had already left for New York and the other was relocating to Raleigh-Durham. It seemed to him that everyone in DC was on the way to another place.

"If only we had our house," Doramae sighed, "we'd be going home. But there is nothing left for us in New Orleans."

Valéry was reminded of the miracle that preserved his family home. "I'm glad I got to meet you and to see your art, Doramae." Valéry was barely able to hide his sadness. He wished he could see Doramae and her grandmother again to talk more about life in New Orleans.

"The opera is rehearsing," Grandmother Marietta said, hoping to lift the melancholy. "I love the opera."

Faint strains of the famous "Habanera," from *Carmen,* came from the stairwell.

"I used to attend opening nights at the Houston Opera," Valéry reminisced. "I've not seen any operas in DC. There's been no one to go with me." He hoped his lament had not sounded like self-pity. His new friends had suffered greatly. His personal problems were insignificant by comparison.

"You must go the opera, mon cher," Marietta said. "They are performing my favorite opera, *Rigoletto.*"

Valéry was not fond of Verdi. He had once seen *Il Trovatore* with an inferior cast and since then avoided Verdi's music.

Marietta opened her large cloth purse and rummaged through bundles of papers. She found an envelope and handed it to Valéry. "This is a discount for the opera. A nice young man gave this to me the other day. He came to see Doramae's art." She winked at Doramae. Valéry suspected that the "nice young man" may have come to see more than the paintings.

"Oh, but I couldn't possibly," Valéry protested. "This is yours."

"Mon ami! I will not be here after tomorrow and cannot use it. I am happy to share this with someone who admires my granddaughter's art." She looked at Luchen with kind eyes. "You'll let your père go to the opera, won't you, mon cher?"

Luchen ambled toward Marietta and licked her hand in agreement.

"Between Grandmamma and Luchen," Doramae said, "you have no choice."

Valéry blushingly agreed. "I'll be happy to attend the opera, Mrs. Cantrelle."

Marietta lifted her arm and offered Valéry the back of her hand. Valéry bent down and provided a gentlemanly kiss. Marietta's face erupted in a mass of wrinkles. "I didn't think you'd do it," she giggled. "So old-fashioned, mon cher."

"Mine is an ancient family." Valéry confessed. "We were Montblanc, but an ancestor shortened it to Blanc a few generations ago."

Marietta drifted into reverie. She recalled meeting a Louisa Blanc, but she didn't mention it to Valéry. Montblanc was a name familiar to everyone back home, a family stretching to the time of Napoleon. "I am honored by your affection," Marietta said, gently caressing the back of her hand where Valéry had placed his kiss.

Valéry thanked Doramae and Marietta for the fine conversation, and the opportunity to see *Rigoletto,* and left the premises. Talking with Doramae and Marietta had engendered a deep sense of nostalgia. He had come east hoping to establish a new life, but he missed his old one. He understood how to relate to people back home. The DC area felt cold and impersonal. Valéry thought about the family reunions and the summer cookouts, the Saturday afternoons shooting the breeze with uncles and cousins, talking about everything and nothing. They were pleasant memories.

Would the family—would Louisa—truly reject him if he revealed the truth about himself? Merely asking the question within the privacy of his own thoughts brought a sense of dread. Yes, they would. He was sure of it.

Valéry looked in the mirror and studied his sagging jowls. His forehead was a farm of deep furrows. His stomach protruded foreword to the point that, when he stood at the toilet, he could not see over the bulge. Valéry had long since ceased grooming what little hair was left, preferring to keep it trimmed short. This was the character who went out prospecting for a lover, expecting Mr. Right to show up while walking his dog. As he examined the weary countenance, he asked the same question he had asked for years: Would he say yes if that man in the mirror asked him on a date? He could not bring himself to answer.

Perhaps the opera would provide escape from his torment. It would be strange, though, going alone. He had usually taken a niece or nephew with him when he attended the opera in Houston. Valéry enjoyed being the uncle that introduced the younger generation to Philip Glass and Leoš Janáček. He'd taken one nephew to see a strange Michael Tippett opera, and now, grown up, that nephew was composing film scores in Hollywood. Valéry took pride in having been the one to expand his horizons.

Memories of his various philanthropies flooded Valéry's thoughts. Perhaps to his young kin, being "the bachelor uncle" meant that he spent time with them when others were too exhausted to pay attention. Valéry had never before thought of it as a term of endearment. The word "bachelor" had always seemed like an indictment.

But if he must go alone to the opera, Valéry decided to look his best. He purchased a fashionable Versace suit and a pair of Italian-made shoes. The dog walker who came during the day didn't work evenings. Luchen would have to be boarded at the vet. The Metro was unpredictable so late at night, and Valéry didn't want to come home to an accident on the rug.

At the Foggy Bottom Metro station, Valéry took the shuttle to the Kennedy Center, arriving with plenty of time to spare. He browsed the gift shop and purchased a facsimile of the pen John F. Kennedy used to sign legislation into law. When he saw a pair of earrings fashioned on ones worn by Jackie, he bought them for Palmyra, a gift he knew she would adore. A signed photograph of JFK was Palmyra's prized possession.

Twenty minutes before the opera was to begin, Valéry entered the orchestra section and was led to his row by an usher. Only one person had taken a seat in the section; it was a young man who appeared to be in his early twenties. Surely the youth was not by himself, Valerie mused. His date must have momentarily excused herself.

Valéry stood in the aisle waiting for the young man's companion to return. He didn't want to take his seat and face an uncomfortable situation where he didn't know if he should strike up a conversation. Within a few minutes, a man and woman entered the row. Valéry now felt comfortable to take his seat. He excused himself as he squeezed past the man and woman, reading the numbers on the back of the chairs as he compared them with his ticket. His seat was next to the young man's. Other couples approached from the opposite direction and, soon, all the seats were taken.

At the first intermission, Valéry rushed to the lobby to get a glass of wine at the liquor kiosk. He tried to focus on the grand drama of the opera, the engaging story of the moral jester entertaining men whom he despised, licentious men who molested young girls. No matter how hard he tried, Valéry kept wondering about the anonymous young man who sat beside him.

Chimes alerted everyone that the second act was about to begin. As he made his way back to the row, Valéry saw that the young man was standing in the aisle. How kind of him to wait so that the people already seated would only be disturbed once.

The end of the second act brought another intermission. This time, Valéry stayed in his seat. So did the young man.

"I've never had a complete recording of *Rigoletto*," Valéry said, "but I must have heard every song."

"Is that so?" the young man said after a long pause.

Valéry turned toward him. "This is so much better than the last Verdi opera I saw."

"I've always liked opera," the young man said.

Valéry wondered how long "always" could possibly be. Upon close inspection, Valéry was not sure the young man had even reached his twenties.

"My name is Valéry."

"I'm Trevor," the young man said.

Valéry offered his hand, and Trevor shook it. Valéry tried to assess the grip. Could a person tell sexual orientation from a handshake?

The awkward moment ended as the lights dimmed for the final act. Rigoletto's pain at finding that his daughter had been abducted, possibly raped, and that she still loved the licentious duke seemed believable to Valéry. He was not surprised at the evil consequences. Rigid constraints placed on the power of love was exactly what kept him from his Louisiana clan.

At the final curtain call, Valéry began to worry that he might lose a chance that he'd later regret. He better let Trevor know how to contact him. He half expected a Rigoletto in the audience to protest his move as he took a card from his wallet and prepared to write down his number. Suddenly, he couldn't go through with it and returned the card to his wallet. The age difference was simply too great. Trevor surely would view his advance as an unpleasant ending to an otherwise splendid entertainment.

Valéry rushed out of the Kennedy Center to catch the first shuttle to the Metro. He took a seat at the rear and lost himself in a sense of despair. He had been unexpectedly overwhelmed by the encounter with Trevor. Though painfully aware of his age, in the moment he shook Trevor's hand, Valéry had felt remarkably young at heart.

Suddenly, he recognized Trevor, sitting in the seat opposite. Should he acknowledge him? Valéry chose to stare out the window as if he hadn't noticed.

The ride was interminably long. He thought the driver would never make it to the Foggy Bottom station. Valéry hoped he could maintain his nonchalant stance until Trevor left the shuttle. As the passengers filed out, Valéry continued to be aware of Trevor. Several times the young man could have exited, but he just sat there. Finally, Valéry had no choice but to stand and greet him. Politeness dictated that much.

"There you are again," Valéry said, trying to sound as if he genuinely had no idea that Trevor had been on the ride. Valéry's clumsy statement made him feel idiotic.

"You were moving fast," Trevor said with a smile. "I guess you were as eager to get the first bus as I was. There aren't a lot of trains this late at night."

An elderly woman on the shuttle, rising with the aid of a cane, looked directly at Trevor and Valéry, scowling. This was the disapproval that Valéry dreaded, even coming from a stranger.

When Trevor left the shuttle, Valéry assumed he would disappear down the Metro escalator, but Trevor was waiting at the entrance.

"That was an amazing performance, wasn't it?" Valéry said, trying to refrain from sounding too pleased that Trevor had not run off.

Trevor didn't respond. Instead he asked, "Why so somber on the bus?"

The statement caught Valéry off-guard. He was surprised that the young man had noticed his mood, and that he used such an erudite word, not *sad* or *melancholy*, but *somber*.

"The opera had a tragic ending," Valéry said, "I can't stop thinking about it."

They rode the escalator down and passed through the turnstile. Valéry felt sure the young man would go his own way. Surely Trevor was only being polite before. But Trevor stayed with him.

"So, where are you from?" Valéry asked. Given the strength of his growing attraction, he wasn't sure he could manage small talk, but he would try.

"The Midwest," Trevor said, noncommittally.

"I'm from the South," Valéry said. He wondered why neither party was being more specific about his origins. He decided to be clear. "I moved here after Katrina hit New Orleans."

Trevor added a detail to his own story, "I used to attend the Lyric Opera in Chicago."

"Is that where you're from?"

"Well, a suburb of Chicago."

"I have to ask," Valéry ventured. "How old are you?"

The young man grinned. "I'm thirty. You probably thought I was younger, right?"

"Well, you do look youthful."

"I guess I am aging well," Trevor said with a grin.

Valéry wasn't sure he believed Trevor about his age, but he didn't want to pursue the issue. "What brought you to DC?"

"We came because of work," Trevor responded.

Valéry almost asked if Trevor was using the royal *we*, or if it referred to a lover. "I came here because of work, also," Valéry volunteered. "I've had a hard time meeting people in DC. And even when I do, they move away."

"I've noticed that, too," Trevor said. "People come and go, don't they? No one has roots here."

"It was strange attending the opera alone," Valéry said, hoping to tease from Trevor the reason he was not with anyone. "I'm not sure I'll do it again."

Trevor didn't comment.

"If you find yourself planning to come alone again to the opera," Valéry added, "perhaps we could come together." He smiled nervously, recognizing what an inane way he had asked Trevor on a date.

Trevor smiled but didn't say anything.

Valéry took out his wallet and found the card he had intended to give Trevor before. It was from the gallery where he had met Marietta.

"Perhaps you'd like to visit this place," Valéry proposed. "I met a New Orleans artist there." Valéry wrote his phone number on the back of the card and, without comment, handed it to Trevor.

Trevor took the card. "I might do that. Most of my friends are, well, Broadway music queens. They won't go to operas, but they will go see art."

Valéry noted the gay word *queens*.

The lights at the edge of the opposite platform began to flash. "That's my train," Trevor said.

Valéry thought he heard disappointment in Trevor's voice. He shook Trevor's hand and said, "Perhaps we can meet again at a gallery opening."

"I'd like to see that gallery. We need some paintings."

There was that word again: *we*.

Valéry watched Trevor get on the metro, but didn't see where he was sitting when it pulled away from the station. Valéry had no idea what he should be feeling.

On the train headed to Takoma Park, Valéry read the synopsis of *Rigoletto*. He scoured the section about Verdi's career and paid close attention to the performance history—anything to keep his mind off Trevor.

When he arrived at his apartment, he found a FedEx package sitting on the floor downstairs by the mailboxes. It had been delivered to the rental office during the day, but the manager always dropped off residents' packages as a courtesy. The return address was his Baton Rouge house, and he recognized Palmyra's scrawl. He knew immediately what it was. Palmyra had mentioned the last time they spoke that she wanted to send the thermos of Sazerac she had promised long ago.

Walking the stairs to his apartment, Valéry opened the box and first found a card with ten dollars in it. Palmyra had written a note saying, "Come home to Dixie when you can, mon cher." He loved his great-aunt. He unscrewed the top of the metal thermos and poured out a drink even before he reached his landing. It was Palmyra's brew all right. He recognized the distinctive edge—not sweet like the ones served in New Orleans bars.

Valéry opened his door and immediately noticed the red light flashing on his answering machine. His heart jumped, but then he realized that it couldn't be Trevor, not this quickly. Valéry pressed the rewind button and listened to a couple of messages left by people from the office. Then he heard his mother's voice.

"Your aunt Palmyra died this evening. Please call when you get this message, Valéry. The family needs you."

Valéry collapsed onto the chair beside his desk, loosened his tie, and replayed the message. He went to the kitchen and got a crystal goblet from the shelf.

"This is to you, Aunt Palmyra," he said, toasting the answering machine that had given him the sad news.

Valéry waited until the last minute before deciding what to do. He could not stop hoping that Trevor would contact him. He was so anxious not to miss a call that he forwarded his home phone to the office.

Two days passed. Valéry began to wonder how he could have allowed himself to be drawn into such fantasies. People don't meet a lover by chance—not like that, not when there are such differences in age and appearance.

Louisa was planning a traditional funeral. Uncle Jacques took over the arrangements. He knew what his sister would want. He invited everyone from miles around to a huge barbecue. They'd take the casket to the park and use it as the table from which to serve everyone. The family never let anyone pass without an unusual send-off.

Valéry told his mother that if he returned, she would have to get used to having a dog around. Valéry boarded Luchen and arranged for a pet carrier to pick him up and ship him on a flight to New Orleans so he would arrive the same day as Valéry. He wanted to travel by bus to give himself a chance to collect his thoughts, to reflect on the time he had spent away from New Orleans.

Closing his bedroom door for the last time, Valéry looked in the dresser mirror. It turned into a movie screen. He saw himself in bed with Trevor, romping under the covers, laughing, in love. Then the image of Trevor rolled to one side, and Valéry found himself looking into his own eyes. He quickly turned off the lights and shut the door.

"The family needs you," Louisa had said.

Valéry signed heavily as the bus left the Peter Pan terminal near Union Station. Going home meant being loved, not as a gay man, but as the adored bachelor uncle. "That will be enough," Valéry told himself. He smiled as the bus rolled through Evangelical Virginia, the Baptist hollows of Kentucky and Tennessee, and then past the Pentecostal Mississippi delta, finally crossing Lake Pontchartrain into the reviving city of New Orleans that he would again call home, to be greeted by the loving embrace of his nieces and nephews, but not by Trevor.

ABOUT THE AUTHOR

William Poe is the author of *Simon Says*, winner of the 2013 International Book Awards in the category Fiction: Gay and Lesbian. His other novel, *Simple Simon*, was also a finalist for the 2013 Book of the Year Award in the category Fiction: Gay and Lesbian.

Poe studied art at the University of Arkansas-Little Rock and anthropology at the University of Nebraska-Lincoln. He is also the author of the acclaimed poetry collection *Myths and Rhymes*.

Made in the USA
Las Vegas, NV
04 October 2021

31687523R00066